PARTNERSHIP
Sharing *the* Vision—Sharing *the* Grace

KENNETH COPELAND

KENNETH
COPELAND
PUBLICATIONS

Unless otherwise noted, all scripture is from the *King James Version* of the Bible.

Scripture quotations marked *The Amplified Bible* are from *The Amplified Bible,* Old Testament © 1965, 1987 by The Zondervan Corporation. *The Amplified Bible New Testament* © 1958, 1987 by The Lockman Foundation. Used by permission.

Partnership
Sharing the Vision—Sharing the Grace

ISBN 1-57562-247-5   30-0059

10 09 08 07 06 05   10 9 8 7 6 5 4

© 1998 Kenneth Copeland Ministries, Incorporated

Kenneth Copeland Publications
Fort Worth, Texas 76192-0001

For more information about Kenneth Copeland Ministries, call 1-800-600-7395 or visit www.kcm.org.

Table of Contents

Introduction

One time, in a monthly Partner letter, I asked my Partners to send me their photographs. Within weeks, more than 32,000 photographs of people from across the United States and around the world lined the walls of our ministry headquarters! It was quite a sight.

As we looked at those faces we had never seen before, Gloria and I were thrilled to see all the people who stood behind us, prayed for us and believed God with us. We rejoiced to realize that each photo represented someone who prayed, who loved God with all their heart. Every one of them was someone for whom the Word of God redirected the course of their lives.

It would be too easy to look at walls filled with photos like that and see only dollar signs—like a sports event promoter would who didn't see the people in the stands, but only the numbers of tickets, parking passes and concessions sold. Any organization can get so caught up in the advancement of the vision that they no longer see the people who are helping bring that vision to pass.

That is why as I looked at those photographs, I rejoiced in the work God had done in me to let me see the faces. I thanked God that I shared a relationship with my Partners that had been developed through the principles of His Word. I was blessed to know that the relationship we shared was developed free of any efforts or initiation on my part based on my needs or the needs of my ministry. Our relationship was based on each of us obeying personal direction from God to be knitted together in His ministry through Kenneth Copeland Ministries.

Don't think that happened overnight.

Before I could ever believe God for men and women who would be Partners with Gloria and me in ministry, I first had to develop my own relationship in partnership with God. The day He called me into a full-time ministry that was to be worldwide in scope, Gloria and I did not even have enough money to get out of town! But in His covenant of partnership with me, God told me three things. One, we would never ask a man for a place to preach. Two, we would never ask people for money to get us by. And three, we would never ever preach anywhere at any time based on a financial arrangement.

In the months after that, I pressed in to God for a full revelation of what His Word taught about partnership. He began to reveal to me how important partnership with other ministries was to my own personal life and to my ministry.

If God had never revealed to me anything more about the power of partnership, I would gladly contribute to the many ministries we and our Partners have supported through KCM, just because He said so. But God showed me in His Word a relationship was established in my giving—a relationship that linked me directly to the giftings, anointings and revelations He was pouring out on those men and women for ministry.

As I pressed into His Word concerning partnership, God gave me three major messages. He showed me how the law of seedtime and harvest works with the seeds of faith we sow into the good soil of the ministry of His Word. He showed me the special relationship that releases the reward of the prophet to those who support him. And He revealed to me the value of being able to partake of the grace operating in a ministry with which I am a partner.

This book comes from those three revelations about partnership. Those three messages are the motivation for the partnership sessions in each of our major meetings. These three principles are foundations for my daily prayers of faith for my Partners. I know they have become partakers of the grace God has bestowed on Gloria and me for ministry. I know they share equally in the rewards—both in heaven and on earth—that God pours out on this ministry. I rejoice to take my Partners and their needs before the throne of God.

The revelation behind these three messages is the foundation for my monthly letter—that goes straight from my heart to my Covenant Partners around the world. I pray and sweat over that letter. It is never off my mind. I'm totally committed to it.

That monthly Covenant Partner letter is an expression of ministry that I never had before I was shown the value of ministering directly to my Partners. And it is an outlet like no other ministry voice I have. That just thrills me. It's my way of talking "face to face" with the thousands of men, women and children who are joined hand in hand with Gloria and me in our journey of faith. Whatever personal challenges and victories I am in the middle of, my Covenant Partners know about them. Whatever God is telling me, they are the first to know. I would estimate that more than ninety-five percent of what I preach in our meetings comes out of the revelation God gives me in my monthly ministry letter to my Partners.

You can see I take partnership as a very sacred thing. I am convinced the principles of partnership work just as powerfully today as they did when Paul wrote his partners at Philippi, "...I have you in my heart; inasmuch as both in my bonds, and in the defence and confirmation of the gospel, *ye all are partakers of my grace*" (Philippians 1:7). I am also convinced that the principles of partnership are the key to victory in these last days. They relate directly to supernatural increase, maximum effectiveness in the end-time harvest and the coming together of the Body of Christ in unity and full manifestation of the ministry gifts in the Church.

The Body of Christ will absolutely explode with power as believers walk in the resources and the power available to them as partners in ministry. As they take hold by faith of the anointings on that ministry with which they are partners, everyone involved in that ministry becomes fully supplied, lacking nothing. Spiritually, they share the full scope of the Anointing of God. Materially, they receive exceeding, abundantly above what they can ask or think!

As you read these messages, you will discover why one of our great joys in life is to pray daily for our friends who have become Partners. We pray not because of something we need, but because we want them to have the good things we know are theirs as a result of their giving (Philippians 4:11, 17).

Let these messages help you renew your mind to everything the Word has to say concerning partnership. Discover and enjoy the last-days power that is at your disposal as a partner in ministry.

Kenneth Copeland

———✦———

The Prophet's Reward

"...As his part is that goeth down to the battle,
so shall his part be that tarrieth by the stuff:
they shall part alike."

1 Samuel 30:24

"He that receiveth a prophet in the name of a prophet
shall receive a prophet's reward; and he that receiveth a
righteous man in the name of a righteous man shall
receive a righteous man's reward. And whosoever shall
give to drink unto one of these little ones a cup of cold
water only in the name of a disciple, verily I say unto you,
he shall in no wise lose his reward."

Matthew 10:41-42

If you've been needing greater faith, more anointing or increase in some area of your life, I want you to study very closely what I'm about to tell you. I don't want you to just read it lightly and take my word that it's true. I want you to get out your Bible and let the Holy Spirit reveal it to you personally.

Here's why. If you will believe and act on the principles you're about to see, you will tap into a spiritual gold mine. It is a mine so deep, so rich, you will never be able to plumb the depths of it in this lifetime. Obviously, I can only scratch the surface of it here. But if you'll spend some time on your own, digging around in it, you'll realize as I have that the power of partnership is greater than anything you'd ever imagined.

"Partnership?" you ask.

Yes, partnership!

You see, contrary to what many people have thought, partnership is not a new idea some fundraiser cooked up. It is an ordinance of God that began in the Old Testament and continued in the New. It is a system, designed by God, to dramatically increase the abilities, resources and rewards of every believer.

That system was officially established and recognized as an ordinance of God in 1 Samuel 30. There we find David and the men who fought under his command in hot pursuit of the Amalekites who had plundered their homes and taken captive their families.

In order to overtake their enemy, David's men had embarked on a grueling military maneuver known as a forced march. That's a march under pressure which involves moving the most men and equipment as far and as fast as possible, while remaining battle-ready at all times. It's a tough assignment, and by the time David's men reached the brook Besor, 200 of them were too exhausted to go on.

David instructed the weary ones to remain behind and guard the supplies. Then he and the rest of the men went on across, found the Amalekites, and by the power of God jerked the slack out of them! They not only defeated the army and recovered all their own possessions, they took what belonged to the Amalekites as well. So when they came back across the Besor, they brought with them great spoil!

When the fighting men rejoined the 200 others, however, some of them didn't want to share the rewards of that war with those who had stayed behind. "...Because they went not with us, we will not give them aught of the spoil that we have recovered," they said (1 Samuel 30:22).

It was at that moment that David, a man after God's own heart, officially established the principle of partnership. He said:

Ye shall not do so, my brethren, with that which the Lord hath given us....*but as his part is that goeth down to the battle, so shall his part be that tarrieth by the stuff: they shall part alike.* And it was so from that day forward, that he made it a statute and an ordinance for Israel unto this day (verses 23-25).

What Can I Do for You, Partner?

You may think that ordinance doesn't mean much for you. But it does. After all, you're a soldier just like David's men were. You are a part of the army of Jesus the Anointed One. You're on a mission to occupy this earth and enforce the devil's defeat until Jesus returns.

You may not be on the front lines of the fivefold

ministry. You may not hold the office of an apostle, prophet, evangelist, pastor or teacher. But if you're in partnership with a minister who is doing the work of God, fighting alongside him or her through prayer or through giving, you'll receive an eternal reward for every person who is born again, and for every believer who is strengthened or healed or delivered as a result of that minister's endeavors.

This year alone, for example, millions of people made Jesus the Lord of their lives through the out-reaches of Kenneth Copeland Ministries and, as a Partner, God is giving you credit for every one of them. Why is that? It's because just like the soldiers who stayed and guarded the stuff, you did your part. You prayed. You gave. You helped us by joining your faith with ours. So as far as God is concerned, you deserve to be rewarded just as much as Gloria and I do because your part is just as important as ours!

"Well, I'd like to believe that, Brother Copeland, but that was an Old Testament ordinance. Are you sure it's still in effect today?"

Yes! Jesus taught the first twelve disciples about it. He reaffirmed to them that principle of partnership by saying:

He that receiveth a prophet in the name of a prophet shall receive a prophet's reward; and he that receiveth a righteous man in the name of a righteous man shall receive a righteous man's reward. And whosoever shall give to drink unto one of these little ones a cup of cold water only in the name of a disciple, verily I say unto you, he shall in no wise lose his reward (Matthew 10:41-42).

It would be sufficiently exciting if the reward we received from our partnership in God's work were strictly a heavenly reward. But, praise God, it's not!

There's also an earthly aspect to this reward system. Partnership is one of God's ways of providing for us, here and now, blessings so great we could never muster up enough faith to receive them on our own.

You can see what I mean if you'll read 2 Kings 4. There you'll find the account of a Shunammite woman who decided to support the ministry of the prophet Elisha. She was so determined to be a partner in his work that one day when he was passing by, she "constrained him to eat bread" (verse 8). She just wouldn't take no for an answer. She insisted that he stay for dinner.

She didn't stop with that, either. She and her husband built a special room onto their house so Elisha would have a place to stay whenever he was in town.

Do you know what Elisha did in return? He called in his servant Gehazi and said, "Go find out what I can do for this woman. Find out what she wants."

So Gehazi went, checked out the situation, then came back and told Elisha:

Verily she hath no child, and her husband is old. And [Elisha] said, Call her. And when he had called her, she stood in the door. And he said, About this season, according to the time of life, thou shalt embrace a son. And she said, Nay, my lord, thou man of God, do not lie unto thine handmaid (verses 14-16).

Obviously this woman didn't have the faith to believe God for a child because when Elisha told her she would bear a son, she said, "No way! You may be a prophet, but you're lying to me now!" That was out there beyond what she could ask or think.

But Elisha didn't have any trouble believing for it, and since she was due a reward and they were in partnership with one another, he just released his faith on her behalf. Sure enough, by the next year that Shunammite woman had a baby.

Take Advantage of the Privileges

That same principle will operate for you today just like it did for her. If you're a Partner with Gloria and me, for example, you've joined with our faith. Now when we started out, we just had enough faith to keep our old car running so we could get from one meeting to the next. But over the years, as this ministry has grown, we've learned how to believe for the millions of dollars it takes to pay television bills and salaries, buy equipment and such.

If you're newer to this faith life than we are, or if you haven't had the opportunities to grow in it that we have, you may have some needs that are out beyond your faith range right now. For example, you might have $50,000 worth of debt you want to pay.

You know God *can* do it, but at this point in your life, it may be hard for you to believe He will do it for *you*.

Well, take advantage of the privileges of partnership. Believing for $50,000 worth of debt reduction isn't hard for Gloria and me. As I said, we have to believe for millions every month. So write that $50,000 debt-reduction prayer request on the sheet I send you every month with my letter, and send it back. Use it as a way to release your faith in the God-ordained power of partnership.

That's why I put that sheet in there. I don't do it just because it's the traditional thing to do. I'm energizing you to take part in the prophet's reward! We have a whole prayer staff here who pray over those requests. Plus, Gloria and I pray for our Partners every day just like we pray for our own family. We're exercising our faith on your behalf, so reach out and receive some of the blessings you have coming to you!

Increase Your Anointing

I want you to realize those blessings aren't limited to this natural, material realm, either. Through partnership, the *anointings* God has given Gloria and me for ministry are also available to you.

The Apostle Paul understood that principle. That's why in the letter to his Philippian partners he had the boldness to say:

I thank my God upon every remembrance of you, always in every prayer of mine for you all making request with joy, for your fellowship [or partnership] in the gospel from the first day until now; being confident of this very thing, that he which hath begun a good work in you will perform it until the day of Jesus Christ: Even as it is meet for me to think this of you all, because I have you in my heart; inasmuch as both in my bonds, and in the defence and confirmation of the gospel, ye all are partakers of my grace (Philippians 1:3-7).

Notice in that last phrase he said, Ye are "partakers of my grace." Not God's grace, my grace! In other words, Paul was saying, "As my partners, you share in the grace God has given me to carry out my ministry."

If you want to see how significant that really is, just read through some of Paul's letters and see the statements he makes about grace. Statements such as, "By the grace of God I am what I am....I laboured more abundantly than they all: yet not I, but the grace of God which was with me" (1 Corinthians 15:10).

Paul was literally telling the Philippians that as his partners, the same anointings that were on him as an apostle had become available to them!

I don't know about you, but I want all the anointing I can get. That's why I'm a partner with the ministries of Oral Roberts, Kenneth Hagin, Jerry Savelle, Jesse Duplantis and many others. I want to be a partaker of their grace!

"But I don't need those kinds of anointings!" you may say. "I'm not a preacher. I'm a mechanic...or a housewife...or a salesman."

That may be your profession, but aren't you called to witness to people, pray for them and minister to them as you go about your daily affairs? Of course you are! And the more of the anointing of God you have available to you, the better you'll be able to do it.

What's more, when you partner up with a ministry, the mechanic anointing, or real estate anointing, or whatever that is on you becomes available to that ministry. When you understand that, you can see when we follow the leadership of the Holy Spirit and come together in partnership as He directs, we'll all be fully supplied. None of us will lack anything. Spiritually, we'll have the full scope of the Anointing of God. And materially we'll enjoy the prophet's reward, joining in faith together to receive exceeding, abundantly above what we can ask or think!

I'm convinced it was that reward Paul had in mind when, in closing his partner letter to the Philippians, he told them, "My God shall supply all your need according to his riches in glory by Christ Jesus!" (Philippians 4:19).

No matter how you look at it, that deal is just too good to pass up. So don't! Make up your mind right now to seek God and find out with whom He wants you to become a partner. Then be like that Shunammite woman and start hunting ways to bless that partner.

You'll have so much fun at it, you'll be tempted to forget all about the reward. But God won't. If you'll keep your faith connected, He'll see to it that you're blessed with more of everything than you ever dreamed possible. He'll see to it that you receive the prophet's reward.

The End-Time Power of Twice-Sown Seed

"While the earth remaineth,
seedtime and harvest...shall not cease."
Genesis 8:22

"Now he that ministereth seed to the sower both
minister bread for your food, and multiply
your seed sown, and increase the fruits of
your righteousness."
2 Corinthians 9:10

"Jesus took the loaves; and when he had
given thanks, he distributed to the disciples,
and the disciples to them that were set down;
and likewise of the fishes as much as they would.
When they were filled, he said unto his disciples,
Gather up the fragments that remain, that nothing
be lost. Therefore they gathered them together, and
filled twelve baskets with the fragments...."
John 6:11-13

For centuries the Church has been absolutely riddled with ungodly ideas concerning prosperity. Financially, the Church has been dominated by the world's system and the world's way of doing business—so much so, in fact, that we actually started preaching it as "God's economics," when God didn't have anything to do with it in the first place.

We brought the world's ways over into the Body of Christ instead of taking the things of God over into the world. But all that has begun to change—and it *is* going to change some more. Big time!

Sowing and Reaping...It's as Old as Dirt

It *must* change because we've come to the end of 2,000 years since Jesus' birth into this earth. Two thousand years of the gospel have been sown into this world, and now it's harvest time. You and I are the ones who will reap this harvest—a harvest like we've never seen before.

But to bring it in, we need to set our thinking straight. We must dig into *God's* principles of economics and begin applying them. And the most fundamental principle of God's economics is the principle of sowing and reaping.

To begin our study of sowing and reaping, let's read an early Old Testament account of it in Genesis 8:20-22:

> Noah builded an altar unto the Lord; and took of every clean beast, and of every clean fowl, and offered burnt offerings on the altar. And the Lord smelled a sweet savour; and the Lord said in his heart, I will not again curse the ground any more for man's sake; for the imagination of man's heart is evil from his youth; neither will I again smite any more every thing living, as I have done. While the earth remaineth, seedtime and harvest, and cold and heat, and summer and winter, and day and night shall not cease.

First, I want to point out that what we just read happened only two verses after Noah stepped off the ark. When Noah and his family left the ark, they were it. There wasn't anyone else. Everything "in whose nostrils was the breath of life" had been wiped out by the Flood (Genesis 7:22).

But God preserved for Himself a seed—Noah and his family, all the fowl, beasts and creeping things—and He planted that seed in the earth and declared, "While the earth remaineth, seedtime and harvest...shall not cease."

So human life on earth began once again from the seed of one man.

The second point I want to make concerning Genesis 8:22 is: "While the earth remaineth, *seedtime* and harvest, and cold and heat, and summer and winter, and day and night shall not cease."

Here, the word *seedtime* is a compound word. It is defined as the season for planting seeds. But if you analyze this word, particularly in the context of this passage of Scripture, I believe you can conclude that this verse is saying, "As long as there is an earth, there will always be a time of planting—and a time of growing—and a time of harvesting."

That makes sense, doesn't it? From the time you plant a crop until the time you harvest it, there's the *growing* time. Right?

We could also say it this way: Seedtime plus growing time equals harvest time.

In the New Testament, Jesus followed through with this concept of seedtime and growing time when the apostles approached Him about increasing their faith.

We read about it in Luke 17:5-6: "The apostles said unto the Lord, Increase our faith. And the Lord said, If ye had faith as a grain of mustard seed, ye might say unto this sycamine tree, Be thou plucked up by the root, and be thou planted in the sea; and it should obey you."

The apostles came to Jesus wanting Him to increase their faith, or to make it grow. But He told them that their faith was like a seed. If *they* would plant it, it would grow. Why? Because faith follows the law of seedtime, growing time and harvest time.

Now I'm purposely introducing this matter of "growing time" because that's what I want us to focus on in just a moment. For now, though, I want to establish in our minds that the primary principle or law of economics in the kingdom of God is this law of sowing and reaping.

Let's look at a very familiar verse of Scripture, Galatians 6:7: "Be not deceived; God is not mocked: for whatsoever a man soweth, that shall he also reap."

Based on the context of this passage, we know that the Apostle Paul is primarily talking about money. But when you examine "Whatsoever a man soweth, that shall he also reap," you realize that this is not just about money. It's a general revelation of the earth's entire operation. In fact, it's the way heaven operates. It's the way the kingdom of God operates. How do we know that?

Well, back there in Genesis 8:22, God declared it as so. Then Jesus said the same thing in Mark 4:30-32.

In Galatians 6, Paul is very aware of this basic law of sowing and reaping and he goes on to apply it to spiritual matters in verse 8: "For he that soweth to his flesh shall of the flesh reap corruption; but he that soweth to the Spirit shall of the Spirit reap life everlasting."

So we see that the law of sowing and reaping is a kingdom law which, consequently, governs the earth and all natural or material matter.

Now, take this basic, yet all-encompassing law of kingdom economics and apply it to this compressed, narrow band of time in which we now live as people of the end times—a time when 6,000 years' worth of God's promises are about to explode all over this earth—and that's when things really start to get interesting.

Pressed for Time

Have you ever noticed how we seem to be a generation of people who are always in a hurry and forever running out of time?

Here we are with all the technology to do anything and everything faster than the speed of light, but we're always out of time. And I can tell you why.

It's because...*we're out of time!*

Remember Amos 9:13? "Behold, the days come, saith the Lord, that the plowman shall overtake the reaper, and the treader of grapes him that soweth seed...."

My friend, this is a picture and prophecy of that end-time harvest we've all been praying and looking for. But watch carefully what is really happening in this verse. (Again, the key is *growing time.*)

How much growing time do you think is involved when the farmer is out in the field, walking a couple of feet behind the guy driving the plow, poking grape seeds in the ground, and then just a few steps behind him is the fellow who's pulling ripe grapes off a mature vine?

I would say the growing time—the span of time from seed to ripe fruit—is only a matter of seconds. But then, that's not even what this scripture is saying.

This verse is actually saying, the plowman, the planter, the reaper and the winemaker are all catching up to one another and passing each other, to the point you cannot tell which one is which.

Is it beginning to look just a little impossible to you?

Well, in the natural it is. But let's find out more about this principle of *growing time,* and how *supernatural* growing time relates to our end-time harvest.

Let's focus our study on John 6:5-13, and start by reading verses 5-9:

> When Jesus then lifted up his eyes, and saw a great company come unto him, he saith unto Philip, Whence shall we buy bread, that these may eat? And this he said to prove him: for he himself knew what he would do. Philip answered him, Two hundred pennyworth of bread is not sufficient for them, that every one of them may take a little. One of his disciples,

Andrew, Simon Peter's brother, saith unto him, There is a lad here, which hath five barley loaves, and two small fishes: but what are they among so many?

Before we read the rest of the passage, I want to stop here and examine these verses so we can get a good idea of what's really happening—what Jesus is saying and how His disciples are responding.

When Jesus looked up and saw the multitude coming, He knew good and well what He was about to do. He also knew class was now in session.

Jesus asked Philip, "Where are we going to buy bread for all these people?"

The Bible is clear: Jesus already knew the answer, but He asked anyway, because—as *The Amplified Bible* says—He wanted to "test" Philip. In other words, Jesus was wanting to get Philip's attention. He wanted to make him think.

Well, how did Philip do?

His response to Jesus was, "Two hundred pennyworth of bread is not sufficient for them, that every one of them may take a little."

I am satisfied that Philip's answer is the very reason Jesus did what He did.

You see, Jesus was—and is—aware of the fact that the way you and I learn is through communication. That's to say, we never really know what we believe until we start hearing our own mouths say it. We may think we have a pretty good handle on some things. But until the pressure gets turned up to the point where words and thoughts start jumping out of our mouths, we never really know what's deep down inside.

How many times have you suddenly found yourself in the middle of a heated argument, saying some things that even shocked you?

Dear God, why did I say that? Where did it come from?

Well, out of the abundance of your heart your mouth spoke—just like Jesus said it would.

So this tells us there is no question as to what Philip had on his mind (and in his heart) that day. *Little.* He had *little* on his mind.

In fact, faced with all those hungry people, *little* was the biggest thing in Philip's eyes. And by that I mean, all he could see at that moment was the problem—*How are we going to feed these folks?* Just getting a few crumbs into these people's hands was far bigger than any answer he could imagine.

Well, along came Andrew and he got in on the test, too. Let's see if he does any better (verses 8-9): "One of his disciples, Andrew, Simon Peter's brother, saith unto him, There is a lad here, which hath five barley loaves, and two small fishes...."

At the start, Andrew did pretty well. He'd been taking notes in class and up to this point, he had heard the Spirit of God enough to realize the answer.

Andrew's problem, however, came when he allowed his own reasoning to talk him out of the answer. He started out in the right direction, but look where he ended up: "There is a lad here, which hath five barley loaves, and two small fishes: but what are they among so many?" His image of the supply turned into crumbs, just like Philip's.

Truthfully, I suspect Andrew never realized that he had tapped into the answer to Jesus' question. Yet, I believe he picked up on it from the Spirit of God. Why else would he bring that little boy with a basket of lunch to Jesus?

In the end, both Philip and Andrew allowed the size of the problem and their own reasoning to block their view of the answer, though it was standing beside them the whole time, staring them in the face.

Twice-Sown Seed

Up to now we've seen how most folks would think in their natural minds about feeding close to 20,000 hungry people with five loaves of bread and two fish.

Now let's watch carefully how Jesus handles this situation. Let's pick up with the rest of that passage of Scripture (John 6:10-13):

> Jesus said, Make the men sit down. Now there was much grass in the place. So the men sat down, in number about five thousand. And Jesus took the loaves; and when he had given thanks, he distributed to the disciples, and the disciples to them that were set down; and likewise of the fishes as much as they would. When they were filled, he said unto his disciples, Gather up the fragments that remain, that nothing be lost. Therefore they gathered them together, and filled twelve baskets with the fragments of the five barley loaves, which remained over and above unto them that had eaten.

On that day, heaven has it recorded that a little boy fed 5,000 men and all their families with two small fish and five loaves of bread.

"Wait, now, Brother Copeland. We just read that Jesus took the bread and fish and distributed them. Didn't Jesus feed those people?"

Oh, Jesus did the miracle and distributed the food, all right. But it wasn't His seed to sow until that lad walked up and handed Him his lunch.

If we will follow closely what happens to that seed, we will be able to understand the significance of this whole event, and the effect of it on our sowing and reaping today.

Matthew 14 records the same event, and in verse 19 we read how Jesus took the seed—the bread and fish—gave thanks for it, blessed it, broke it and gave it to His disciples. Before Jesus did all this, however, He told the disciples, "Bring them hither to me" (verse 18).

Why do you suppose Jesus told the disciples to give Him the bread and fish?

Couldn't He just as easily have said, "Hold them up and let Me bless them?"

Why did Jesus want to *handle* that seed?

The reason was, the anointing of increase.

The anointing of *increase* is literally and figuratively in the hands of the minister, just as it was present in Jesus' hands that day.

Throughout the Bible, we see the anointing of increase in the hands of God's ministry. That's why God instructed Israel in the Old Testament, and Christians in the New Testament, to bring all their tithes, offerings and goods into the ministry.

God's way is for goods to come into the ministry— for the ministry to receive it, handle it, bless it and distribute it, or sow it—then for it to go out, multiplied in greater number than when it came in. That's the anointing of increase.

The Bible says, "Now he that ministereth seed to the sower both minister bread for your food, and multiply your seed sown..." (2 Corinthians 9:10).

When that boy sowed seed into Jesus' ministry, Jesus received it, applied His anointing of increase to it, then turned around and sowed it into His disciples and the multitude. But as the anointing of increase in and on Jesus hit that boy's seed, not only did it cause the seed to multiply, it also did something supernatural to the growing time of that seed.

The "plowman overtook the reaper, and the treader of grapes him that soweth seed." We could say time culminated in Jesus. Optimum results were produced in minimal time. The seed's *growing time* was compressed to the point that the seed multiplied, grew and produced fruit as fast as the people could eat it. Harvest was produced within moments.

That's not where the story ends, though. We haven't seen the real harvest yet!

God could not fulfill His Word—the law of sowing and reaping—to that young fellow until all 20,000 people had eaten and were full. The reason He couldn't was because the boy's seed was sown a second time by Jesus. And when Jesus sowed it, the boy's seed began multiplying, and multiplying and multiplying.

Everything those people ate that day came from that boy's seed. Then after everyone was full, Jesus told His disciples to "gather up the fragments that remain, that nothing be lost" (John 6:12).

Was Jesus being tight or stingy?

No. Those twelve baskets of leftovers belonged to

that boy. They didn't belong to Jesus. Jesus was just making sure He didn't lose any of the boy's harvest.

Notice, however, those baskets of leftovers were only the boy's immediate harvest from having sown directly into Jesus' ministry. The fulfillment of his harvest, the fulfillment of God's obligation to him, was the fruit from seeds multiplied and sown into the lives of nearly 20,000 people.

He fed the multitudes for Jesus and had enough seed to last a lifetime. That's twice-sown seed.

My friend, the twice-sown seed is where you and I need to learn to exercise our faith and keep our expectancy.

Remember how Philip could see only *little*, and how Andrew started off right, but talked himself out of it?

That kind of thinking will not bring in this end-time harvest we have facing us.

We need to line up our thinking with God's anointing. We need to expect His anointing in every situation. After all, God's style is "pressed down, and shaken together, and running over..." (Luke 6:38). That's the way He does things.

God didn't create a corncob with one kernel of corn

on it. He created a corncob with an abundance of kernels on it, and all creation is designed the same way.

We have moved into an era of exceeding, abundantly beyond what we could ask or think, a time when God now has the opportunity for His people to have more than enough to do *all* that He wants us to do, instead of the devil stealing everything as fast as it grows in the field.

Think of all the missionaries who have gone to China, Africa, South America and all those places. They preached, shed their tears and gave their lives, and it looked like the devil had the upper hand.

Well, I have news for you. Every seed sown for the last 2,000 years—every word preached, every tear and drop of blood shed—is coming up...*now!*

All 2,000 years' worth of gospel seed planted is coming up a hundredfold, and we're the ones to bring it in.

It's loaves and fishes time. It's multiply-the-seed time. The plowman and reaper are passing each other until you cannot tell which is which.

Let's get in on God's system of economics and get a net-breaking, boat-sinking load of souls before we leave this place!

Partake of the Grace

"Being confident of this very thing,
that he which hath begun a good work in you
will perform it until the day of Jesus Christ:
Even as it is meet for me to think this of you all,
because I have you in my heart; inasmuch as both
in my bonds, and in the defence and confirmation
of the gospel, ye all are partakers of my grace."
Philippians 1:6-7

"They went forth, and preached every where,
the Lord working with them,
and confirming the word with signs following."
Mark 16:20

"Elijah said unto Elisha,
Ask what I shall do for thee,
before I be taken away from
thee. And Elisha said, I pray thee,
let a double portion of thy spirit
be upon me."
2 Kings 2:9

A few years ago, tornadoes ripped across Central

Texas, causing massive destruction. One tornado hit the little town of Jarrell and nearly wiped it out—and I don't say that just as a figure of speech. Several blocks of houses, including some businesses, were literally flattened.

In fact, just to give you an idea of how violent this tornado was, as meteorologists from the National Weather Service tracked it, they had originally classified it as an F-4, which meant it was a whirlwind of destruction going somewhere to happen. Later, however, they reclassified it as a level F-5 tornado—a severe storm that is rarely ever seen. The funnel-shaped cloud was calculated to be more than half a mile wide, and had surface winds of more than 250 miles per hour. I'm telling you, *that* was a tornado.

Of course, when any sort of local or national disaster like this happens, one of the first things our KCM staff does is pray. But we also check our computers and get on the phones to find out if we have any Partners who have been affected by the disaster, especially pastors and churches. We make every effort to find out what we can do to help them, as well as their communities.

In this case, we learned that we had a Partner right in the middle of that tornado's wide path of destruction.

It took some time, but when we finally got a call through to our Partner in Jarrell, this is what he said: "Tell Kenneth and Gloria we're all right. That tornado got within half a block of our house and we took authority over it. We just started talking to it, and it went around us and on to downtown where it wiped out all the others."

My friend, if there ever were a generation that needed to live and walk in faith and love every moment, it's the generation in which you and I now live. Thank God we have His Word and His powerful anointing. But also thank God we have each other. We need each other! We need each others' faith. We need each others' prayers.

In these days, especially, it is important that we be conected with anointed, praying people, because—as we are about to see—our individual anointings and our individual prayers of faith flowing in one direction are far more powerful than any one of us alone could ever be. They're certainly more powerful than any storm the devil might throw our way, which is how God intended it to be.

Knocking the Wind out of a Storm

Gloria and I are privileged and honored to have more than 280,000 anointed, praying and believing Partners around the world who have joined their faith and their love with Kenneth Copeland Ministries. These are believers who are committed to support KCM in every way the Spirit of God leads them.

I don't mind telling you that it's a great source of joy and strength just knowing that all 280,000 Partners are out there standing strong with us, wherever we might be in the world, facing whatever storms we might have to face. After all, it takes far more than what Gloria and I have in order to get the message of victory in Jesus into the hands of God's people. It takes partnership!

For the past 36 years of ministry, we have been like the Apostle Paul, who, when he wrote to his partners, said:

I thank my God in all my remembrance of you. In every prayer of mine I always make my entreaty and petition for you all with joy

(delight). [I thank my God] for your fellowship (your sympathetic cooperation and
contributions and partnership) in advancing
the good news (the Gospel) from the first day
[you heard it] until now (Philippians 1:3-5,
The Amplified Bible).

Sure, the list of KCM Partners is long—and actually, it's about to get even longer, because the Spirit
of God recently told Gloria and me that we will have
one million Partners—*and we will!* But that list of
names, however long it may be, is not just set up to
be some marketing tool for us to use when we
decide to mail something.

No, that list of names represents real, flesh-and-
blood, Holy Ghost-anointed people who are in
covenant with us—and with each other—helping
us serve the God of Covenant. Gloria and I hold
these precious souls in our hearts every moment
of every day. Not a day goes by that we don't pray
for our Partners, using a list of specific scriptures
that the Lord has given us to pray, *and believe,* on
their behalf.

You see, when Paul wrote this letter to his partners

in Philippi, he wasn't just scratching out some nice words to make them feel all warm and good about themselves. No, he was explaining some very important spiritual principles where ministry was concerned. He was explaining the exchange, or two-way flow, of God's grace and power in partnerships established for the purpose of ministry.

Certainly, prayer is a major part of this partnership exchange, and it is the focus of our study. But Paul was saying that there was even more being transferred in the exchange. We read about it in Philippians 1:6-7:

Being confident of this very thing, that he which hath begun a good work in you will perform it until the day of Jesus Christ: Even as it is meet for me to think this of you all, because I have you in my heart; inasmuch as both in my bonds, and in the defence and confirmation of the gospel, ye all are partakers of my grace.

Basically, Paul was telling his partners, "Hey, we're in this together. And the grace—or anointings—that God put on me, He has put on you by having joined us together. So expect every anointing and blessing that I have operating in my life to operate in yours as well!"

Remember our Partner in Jarrell, Texas?

There's no telling how many times I prayed for that one Partner as I lifted my hands toward heaven and said, "Father, I pray for my Partners...," and then went through all the scriptures I pray, and ended by praying in other tongues.

In fact, one of the scriptures I pray for my Partners is Psalm 91 which says, "A thousand shall fall at thy side, and ten thousand at thy right hand; but it shall not come nigh thee" (verse 7).

Do you see the benefit of that scripture prayed for this man and his home?

But it doesn't stop there!

Think of all the other 280,000 Partners around the world praying for this man. Think of all the KCM staff around the world praying for this man—all of us praying, agreeing and joining our faith with scriptures such as Psalm 23: "Yea, though I walk through the valley of the shadow of death, I will fear no evil: for thou art with me..." (verse 4); Psalm 103: "Who redeemeth thy life from destruction..."

(verse 4); Isaiah 54: "No weapon that is formed against thee shall prosper..." (verse 17).

Just imagine that F-5 tornado whirling itself right up to our Partner's street in Jarrell, but then having to go around it because of the 280,000 praying, anointed and faith-filled Partners.

I guarantee you that partnership—corporate prayers, corporate anointings, corporate faith—is what turned a storm of that magnitude away!

My point is, it is important for us to understand, where covenant partnership is concerned, that when you pray for me, you're praying for Gloria. When you pray for Gloria, you're praying for me. When you pray for us, you're praying for a Partner in Jarrell, Texas, and others around the world. And when Gloria and I pray for them, we're praying for you.

Do you see the exchange and flow of prayer and anointing? Do you see the strength of it?

That's how God designed it. That's what partnership is all about. It's about partaking of each others' grace.

Behind Every Good Preacher...

As we study the wealth of spiritual instruction Paul left behind in his writings to his New Testament partners, I believe there is a subtle mind-set from which we must guard ourselves. I say *subtle,* yet, over centuries this mind-set has developed into a stronghold of religious tradition.

The mind-set I'm referring to is the one that says, "Oh, sure, Brother Copeland, it's nice to think we can partake of each others' grace. But, let's face it, back then, that was *the Apostle Paul,* handpicked by Jesus Himself."

In other words, we must guard ourselves from putting Paul—or any other Church leader, for that matter—up on a spiritual pedestal and labeling his life and ministry as "Unrealistic for Me Today." Let me show you what I mean.

Again, let's pick up with Paul's letter to his partners in Philippi by reading Philippians 1:19-20:

> For I know that this shall turn to my salvation through your prayer, and the supply of the Spirit of Jesus Christ [the Anointed One], according to my earnest expectation and my hope, that in nothing I shall be ashamed, but

that with all boldness, as always, so now also Christ [the Anointed One and His Anointing] shall be magnified in my body, whether it be by life, or by death.

Here, it's obvious to us that Paul earnestly expected his partners to pray and stand with him, so he could do what he had been called by God to do. He expected his partners to covenant with him, to join with him and undergird him with prayer. It was those prayers that were so vital to Paul's ministry because they were his connection to an even greater supply of the Spirit—a greater supply of anointing which was necessary to get the job done. The prayers of all those believers who were Paul's partners were his connection to their corporate anointings.

Consequently, if Paul's partners did not pray and daily hold him up the way he was holding them up daily, there was a definite possibility failure could be at his doorstep. The exchange, or flow of prayer and anointing, would be hindered.

You mean to say that Paul could have failed?

That's right. Paul could have failed.

By writing what he did to the church at Philippi,

he was acknowledging that, without the prayers and support of his partners, "I will be ashamed before God, because I won't be able to complete all that I am supposed to do. By myself I will fall short."

Now, to prove even further this point of Paul's reliance upon the prayers and support of his partners, let's take one aspect of Paul's ministry to see how this partnership exchange applies. Let's look at his *boldness*.

When we think of the Apostle Paul, we might often think of the boldness demonstrated throughout his life and ministry. After all, we see in the New Testament that he was a very bold man. There were times when he would get right up in the faces of kings and high officials, point his finger at them and say, "You will not get away with this!" And they didn't.

Certainly, we could attribute Paul's boldness to his keen awareness of his position of authority as a born-again child of God in the Anointed Jesus. Nevertheless, there was something uncommon about his boldness.

So, where exactly did he get this uncommon boldness?

To answer that question, let's read a portion of a letter Paul wrote to another group of partners. It's found in Ephesians 6:10-20:

Finally, my brethren, be strong in the Lord, and in the power of his might. Put on the whole armour of God, that ye may be able to stand against the wiles of the devil. For we wrestle not against flesh and blood, but against principalities, against powers, against the rulers of the darkness of this world, against spiritual wickedness in high places. Wherefore take unto you the whole armour of God, that ye may be able to withstand in the evil day, and having done all, to stand. Stand therefore, having your loins girt about with truth, and having on the breastplate of righteousness; And your feet shod with the preparation of the gospel of peace; Above all, taking the shield of faith, wherewith ye shall be able to quench all the fiery darts of the wicked. And take the helmet of salvation, and the sword of the Spirit, which is the word of God: Praying always with all prayer and supplication in the Spirit, and watching thereunto with all perseverance and supplication for all saints; And for me, that utterance may be given unto me, that I may open my mouth boldly, to make known the mystery of the gospel, For which I am an ambassador in bonds: that therein I may speak boldly, as I ought to speak.

First, notice the connection Paul makes here between prayer and boldness. He tells his partners to put on the whole armor of God and assume a position of offensive attack through prayer. Then he tells them, "And while you're praying, pray that I might have *boldness* and utterance."

Notice, too, that once again Paul is asking his partners—this time, the church at Ephesus—to pray for him to have boldness. And once again, he is acknowledging that the prayers of his partners have everything to do with his anointing to speak boldly the mystery of the gospel. There is definitely a pattern here—but there's even more.

As with his partners in Philippi, Paul not only asked his partners in Ephesus to pray, he *expected* them to pray. And by their prayers, he fully *expected* the Holy Spirit to supply him with all the boldness he needed. It was no different than his fully expecting to be supplied with all the finances he needed. It

was no different than his fully expecting to be supplied with all the anointings he needed.

For Paul's boldness to be at the level he needed it to
be in order to declare the mystery of the gospel in any
situation, at any time, he needed his partners' prayers.
Of course, the actual boldness came from the Spirit of
God, but it was his partners' prayers of agreement that
helped magnify that boldness to a higher level.

Paul knew his partners' prayers were his success.

No Spectators Here!

In all my years as a believer and minister of the
gospel, I have observed how the Church has had a
tendency to stand back and let the *anointed ministers of God* bear most of the weight of responsibility
in carrying out the commandments of Jesus. Too
often we've sat back like an audience, or room full of
spectators, and watched as the pastors, evangelists
and so on, did the work.

My brother and sister, that has never been God's
intention. That is not His way.

Even when Jesus came to this earth to minister,
He came needing help. He came looking for assis-
tance *and* assistants.

When Jesus of Nazareth came up from the waters of the Jordan River, having been baptized by John the Baptist, in that moment the Spirit of the Lord came upon Him and baptized Him for public ministry (John 1:29-34; Luke 4:18-19).

Jesus walked this earth bearing all the anointings of God, being the fullness of God manifested in the flesh. Yet, when He went up from the banks of the Jordan and began His earthly ministry, He chose twelve partners with whom to get started.

Have you ever noticed that every one of Jesus' partners in ministry was a businessman? Every one of them. They knew nothing about ministry, but Jesus needed partners and they were willing to leave the business world to serve Him.

But now let's take that thought a step further. Not only did Jesus need their partnership, but He also needed their prayers, just as we saw with the Apostle Paul's ministry. In Matthew 26 and Mark 14, it is recorded that Jesus went to the garden in Gethsemane, along with His disciples—His partners—to pray.

In perhaps His greatest hour of need, Jesus looked to His partners for their support. He needed their presence. He needed their prayers. Three different times during that spiritual night watch, He indicated that He needed their help. As it turned out, it also happened to be one of the disciples' greatest hours of need, but they gave in to their flesh. They slept.

Today is no different. You and I are in the middle of a night watch, waiting for the return of Jesus, and the Church is in perhaps its greatest hour of need.

If Jesus needed the prayers and support of His partners, if the Apostle Paul needed the prayers and support of his partners, Gloria and I certainly need the prayers and support of our Partners to complete what God has called us to do.

My friend, the Bible says one of us can put a thousand to flight, and two of us, 10,000 to flight (Deuteronomy 32:30). Just imagine what 280,000 KCM Partners are doing right at this moment.

Better yet, imagine what one million will do.

A Prayer for My Partners

Father, I praise You and bless You and thank You for my Partners. Lord, every prayer that's ever been prayed for Gloria and for me and for all of us at Kenneth Copeland Ministries, I thank You for it. I release my faith for them and with them in every area of their lives.

Father, I pray the power of God—the Anointing of God—that is in and on Gloria and me and the corporate anointing that is in and on KCM be in the household and in the ministry and business affairs of every Partner we have. Let this anointing be on them as they minister and as they pray. Let it be on them in the lives of their children to remove the burdens and destroy the yokes, in the Name of Jesus.

Father, there are so many of them, I could not call

individually before the throne of grace every name of every Partner I have. I would if I could. So I'm asking You by the Holy Spirit to enter the individual name of every Partner into these scriptures that I have committed to pray over them every day of my life.

I'm asking You to enter their names into the 23rd Psalm. Lord, You are their Shepherd. They shall not want. You make them lie down by the prospering green fields and lead them beside the still waters.

I believe You for Your peace to rule in their lives. Even though they walk through the valley of the shadow of death, they will fear no evil because You are with them. You have prepared a table before them in the presence of their enemies. You walk with them everywhere they go.

Father, I pray the 91st Psalm and I say of the Lord, You are their refuge and their fortress. You're their God and in You they do trust.

Father, I pray the 103rd Psalm and all of its benefits for my Partners. I thank You that their iniquities are forgiven—they are completely wiped out. Thank You that sickness and disease are taken from their midst, and their youth is renewed like the eagle's. And thank You that the angels of God take up their righteous cause. Hallelujah.

Father, I pray Isaiah 54:8-17 for all of my Partners. Great shall be the peace of their children; in righteousness they shall be established. They shall be far from oppression, for they shall not fear. They shall be far from terror, for it shall not come near them. Thank You, Lord, that no weapon formed against them can prosper.

Father, I pray Ephesians 1:16-23 for them. Thank You that the eyes of their understanding are opened, flooding their spirit with the light of the power of the living God. Reveal to them what is the power toward us who believe that You wrought when You raised Jesus from the dead, and, setting all things under His feet, gave Him to be the head over us who are His Body. We are the Body of the Anointed One. We are the Body of His Anointing. Hallelujah.

Father, I pray Ephesians 3:14-20, thanking You for a revelation that they are strengthened with might by Your Spirit in their spirit, that they comprehend with all the saints what's the length, the breadth, the height and the depth, and to know the love of the Anointed One. I thank You that they overflow with the anointing to love, and that they know and are filled with the fullness of You who are able to do exceeding abundantly above all that we ask or think.

And, I pray Colossians 1:9-13, thanking You for delivering them from the authority of darkness and translating them into the kingdom of Your dear Son, strengthening them with might by Your Spirit in their spirit so they walk worthy of You, Lord. I thank You for it, and I praise You for it.

Now, Satan, I bind you and cast you out.

I plead the blood of Jesus over every person, every family, every household, every business, every ministry, every church that's in partnership with Kenneth Copeland Ministries. God, I praise You and thank You for it. I thank You for my Partners, Lord. Hallelujah. Bless the Lord, O my soul, and forget not all His benefits. Praise You, Jesus.

Now Lord, they have invested their goods, and they have invested time, and they have invested effort, and they have invested prayer into this ministry.

Father, I'm asking You for supernatural harvest to come into their hands—the supernatural harvest of the former and the latter rain coming all at one time—such a harvest that the reapers catch up with the sowers.

I thank You for such a harvest that the moment it's sown, harvest time will be there, and they will reap it and bring it in. Exceeding, abundantly beyond all they even dare ask or think will flow into their lives—great, overflowing abundance of goods, resources, deliverance, healing, miracles—whatever it takes. Sweep their families into the kingdom. Give them the greatest ideas that have ever been born into the earth. Create whole industries from the ideas that You give my Partners.

I thank You for it, Lord. I give You the praise and the glory and the honor for it in the Name of Jesus. I declare with my faith, this year will be the grandest year in human history. Great shall be the peace of the Body of Christ and great shall be the peace of Jerusalem. Not this man-made peace that men are running around all over the world with, but the peace of God that passes all understanding. Peace that rules in the hearts of men, not just in their capital cities, politicians and politics. We'll not have politics as usual this year. I release my faith.

Now, Lord, I make demand on the promises. You

said that You would not have us be ignorant of these end times—that You would not have us be ignorant of Your Word and Your affairs; You would not have us be ignorant of the anointings; You would not have us be ignorant of the seasons and the times that we live in. I ask You for great revelation. I rebuke spiritual ignorance amongst us. I rebuke spiritual ignorance from amongst my Partners. Oh God, I receive the light from heaven—revelation of You, hallelujah.

For every apostle, every prophet, every evangelist, every pastor and every teacher, every Sunday school teacher, every minister of helps who is a Partner to this ministry, I receive revelation. Fill their pulpits with fire from heaven. And I give You the praise and the honor and the glory for it. Glory to God forevermore.

Amen.

Prayer for Salvation and Baptism in the Holy Spirit

Heavenly Father, I come to You in the Name of Jesus. Your Word says, "Whosoever shall call on the name of the Lord shall be saved" (Acts 2:21). I am calling on You. I pray and ask Jesus to come into my heart and be Lord over my life according to Romans 10:9-10: "If thou shalt confess with thy mouth the Lord Jesus, and shalt believe in thine heart that God hath raised him from the dead, thou shalt be saved. For with the heart man believeth unto righteousness; and with the mouth confession is made unto salvation." I do that now. I confess that Jesus is Lord, and I believe in my heart that God raised Him from the dead.

I am now reborn! I am a Christian—a child of Almighty God! I am saved! You also said in Your Word, "If ye then, being evil, know how to give good gifts unto your children: HOW MUCH MORE shall your heavenly Father give the Holy Spirit to them that ask him?" (Luke 11:13). I'm also asking You to fill me with the Holy Spirit. Holy Spirit, rise up within me as I praise God. I fully expect to speak with other tongues as You give me the utterance (Acts 2:4). In Jesus' Name. Amen!

Begin to praise God for filling you with the Holy Spirit. Speak those words and syllables you receive—not in your own language, but the language given to you by the Holy Spirit. You have to use your own voice. God will not force you to speak. Don't be concerned with how it sounds. It is a heavenly language!

Continue with the blessing God has given

you and pray in the spirit every day.

You are a born-again, Spirit-filled believer. You'll never be the same!

Find a good church that boldly preaches God's Word and obeys it. Become a part of a church family who will love and care for you as you love and care for them.

We need to be connected to each other. It increases our strength in God. It's God's plan for us.

Make it a habit to watch the *Believer's Voice of Victory* television broadcast and become a doer of the Word, who is blessed in his doing (James 1:22-25).

About the Author

Kenneth Copeland is co-founder and president of Kenneth Copeland Ministries in Fort Worth, Texas, and best-selling author of books that include *Managing God's Mutual Funds—Yours and His, How to Discipline Your Flesh* and *Honor—Walking in Honesty, Truth and Integrity.*

Now in his 36th year as a minister of the gospel of Christ and teacher of God's Word, Kenneth is the recording artist of such award-winning albums as his Grammy-nominated *Only the Redeemed, In His Presence, He Is Jehovah* and his most recently released *Just a Closer Walk.* He also co-stars as the character Wichita Slim in the children's adventure videos *The Gunslinger, Covenant Rider* and the movie *The Treasure of Eagle Mountain,* and as Daniel Lyon in the *Commander Kellie and the Superkids*_{SM} videos *Armor of Light* and *Judgment: The Trial of Commander Kellie.*

With the help of offices and staff in the United States, Canada, England, Australia, South Africa and Ukraine, Kenneth is fulfilling his vision to boldly preach the uncompromised Word of God from the top of this world to the bottom, and all the way around. His ministry reaches millions of people worldwide through daily and Sunday TV broadcasts, magazines, teaching audios and videos, conventions and campaigns, and the World Wide Web.

Books Available From
Kenneth Copeland Ministries

by Kenneth Copeland

* A Ceremony of Marriage
  A Matter of Choice
  Covenant of Blood
  Faith and Patience—The Power Twins
* Freedom From Fear
  Giving and Receiving
  Honor—Walking in Honesty, Truth and Integrity
  How to Conquer Strife
  How to Discipline Your Flesh
  How to Receive Communion
  In Love There Is No Fear
  Know Your Enemy
  Living at the End of Time—A Time of
      Supernatural Increase
  Love Never Fails
  Managing God's Mutual Funds—Yours and His
  Mercy—The Divine Rescue of the Human Race
* Now Are We in Christ Jesus
  One Nation Under God (gift book with CD enclosed)
* Our Covenant With God
  Partnership, Sharing the Vision—Sharing the Grace
* Prayer—Your Foundation for Success
* Prosperity: The Choice Is Yours
  Rumors of War
* Sensitivity of Heart
* Six Steps to Excellence in Ministry
* Sorrow Not! Winning Over Grief and Sorrow
* The Decision Is Yours
* The Force of Faith
* The Force of Righteousness
  The Image of God in You
* The Laws of Prosperity
* The Mercy of God (available in Spanish only)
  The Outpouring of the Spirit—
      The Result of Prayer
* The Power of the Tongue
  The Power to Be Forever Free
* The Winning Attitude
  Turn Your Hurts Into Harvests
  Walking in the Realm of the Miraculous
* Welcome to the Family
* You Are Healed!
  Your Right-Standing With God

* Available in Spanish

by Gloria Copeland

* And Jesus Healed Them All
  Are You Listening?
  Are You Ready?
  Be a Vessel of Honor
  Build Your Financial Foundation
  Fight On!
  Go With the Flow
  God's Prescription for Divine Health
  God's Success Formula
  God's Will for You
  God's Will for Your Healing
  God's Will Is Prosperity
* God's Will Is the Holy Spirit
* Harvest of Health
  Hidden Treasures
  Living Contact
  Living in Heaven's Blessings Now
  Looking for a Receiver
* Love—The Secret to Your Success
  No Deposit—No Return
  Pleasing the Father
  Pressing In—It's Worth It All
  Shine On!
  The Grace That Makes Us Holy
  The Power to Live a New Life
  The Protection of Angels
  There Is No High Like the Most High
  The Secret Place of God's Protection
      (gift book with CD enclosed)
  The Unbeatable Spirit of Faith
  This Same Jesus
  To Know Him
* Walk in the Spirit (available in Spanish only)
  Walk With God
  Well Worth the Wait
  Words That Heal (gift book with CD enclosed)
  Your Promise of Protection—
      The Power of the 91st Psalm

Books Co-Authored by Kenneth and Gloria Copeland

  Family Promises
  Healing Promises
  Prosperity Promises

Protection Promises

* From Faith to Faith—
   A Daily Guide to Victory
From Faith to Faith—A Perpetual Calendar

One Word From God Can Change Your Life

One Word From God Series:
- One Word From God Can Change Your Destiny
- One Word From God Can Change Your Family
- One Word From God Can Change Your Finances
- One Word From God Can Change
   Your Formula for Success
- One Word From God Can Change Your Health
- One Word From God Can Change Your Nation
- One Word From God Can Change Your Prayer Life
- One Word From God Can Change Your Relationships

Load Up—A Youth Devotional
Over the Edge—A Youth Devotional
Pursuit of His Presence—A Daily Devotional
Pursuit of His Presence—A Perpetual Calendar

Other Books Published by KCP

The First 30 Years—A Journey of Faith
   The story of the lives of Kenneth and Gloria Copeland
Real People. Real Needs. Real Victories.
   A book of testimonies to encourage your faith
John G. Lake—His Life, His Sermons
   His Boldness of Faith
The Holiest of All by Andrew Murray
The New Testament in Modern Speech
   by Richard Francis Weymouth
The Rabbi From Burbank by Rabbi Isidor Zwirn
   and Bob Owen
Unchained by Mac Gober

Products Designed for Today's Children and Youth

And Jesus Healed Them All (confession book and CD gift package)
Baby Praise Board Book
Baby Praise Christmas Board Book

* Available in Spanish

Noah's Ark Coloring Book
The Best of *Shout!* Adventure Comics
The *Shout!* Giant Flip Coloring Book
The *Shout!* Joke Book
The *Shout!* Super-Activity Book
Wichita Slim's Campfire Stories

*Commander Kellie and the Superkids*_{SM} Books:

The SWORD Adventure Book
*Commander Kellie and the Superkids*_{SM}
 Solve-It-Yourself Mysteries
*Commander Kellie and the Superkids*_{SM}
 Adventure Series: Middle Grade Novels
 by Christopher P.N. Maselli:

#1 The Mysterious Presence
#2 The Quest for the Second Half
#3 Escape From Jungle Island
#4 In Pursuit of the Enemy
#5 Caged Rivalry
#6 Mystery of the Missing Junk
#7 Out of Breath
#8 The Year Mashela Stole Christmas

World Offices
of Kenneth Copeland Ministries

For more information about KCM and a free
catalog, please write the office nearest you:

Kenneth Copeland Ministries
Fort Worth, Texas 76192-0001

Kenneth Copeland
Locked Bag 2600
Mansfield Delivery Centre
QUEENSLAND 4122
AUSTRALIA

Kenneth Copeland
Post Office Box 15
BATH
BA1 3XN
U.K.

Kenneth Copeland
Private Bag X 909
FONTAINEBLEAU
2032
REPUBLIC OF
SOUTH AFRICA

Kenneth Copeland
Post Office Box 378
Surrey, B.C.
V3T 5B6
CANADA

Kenneth Copeland Ministries
Post Office Box 84
L'VIV 79000
UKRAINE

Believer's Voice of Victory Television Broadcast

Join Kenneth and Gloria Copeland and the *Believer's Voice of Victory* broadcasts Monday through Friday and on Sunday each week, and learn how faith in God's Word can take your life from ordinary to extraordinary. This teaching from God's Word is designed to get you where you want to be—*on top!*

You can catch the *Believer's Voice of Victory* broadcast on your local, cable or satellite channels.

Check your local listings for times and stations in your area.

Believer's Voice of Victory Magazine

Enjoy inspired teaching and encouragement from Kenneth and Gloria Copeland and guest ministers each month in the *Believer's Voice of Victory* magazine. Also included are real-life testimonies of God's miraculous power and divine intervention in the lives of people just like you!

It's more than just a magazine—it's a ministry.

To receive a FREE subscription to *Believer's Voice of Victory*, write to:

Kenneth Copeland Ministries
Fort Worth, Texas 76192-0001
Or call:
1-800-600-7395
(7 a.m.-5 p.m. CT)
Or visit our Web site at:
www.kcm.org

If you are writing from outside the U.S., please contact the KCM office nearest you. Addresses for all Kenneth Copeland Ministries offices are listed on the previous pages.